Making a Big Sandcastle

Elsie Nelley
Photographs by Lindsay Edwards

Contents

Materials

Here is wet sand for the sandcastle.

Here is a shovel.

Here is a bucket.

Here are
some little sticks.

Here are some big shells
and some little shells.

Here is
a big feather.

Steps

The sandcastle will go here.

This is the bottom
of the sandcastle.

Here is some wet sand.

It goes in the bucket.

The wet sand
is for the top
of the sandcastle.

The top of the sandcastle goes on here.

The sandcastle
looks like this.

Here are some little sticks.

They are for two **doors** on the sandcastle.

Here are some big shells for the **windows**.

The big shells go here.

The little shells are
for the windows, too.

They go here.

This big feather
goes up here.

It is a flag
for the big sandcastle.

Glossary

doors

windows